AF594854

With love to our little angel, Zach
~ Mimi

THE WISE ANIMAL HANDBOOK

Kate B. Jerome

Arcadia Kids

Attempt new skills from time to time.

Just try to think them through.

And if you find you're left behind...

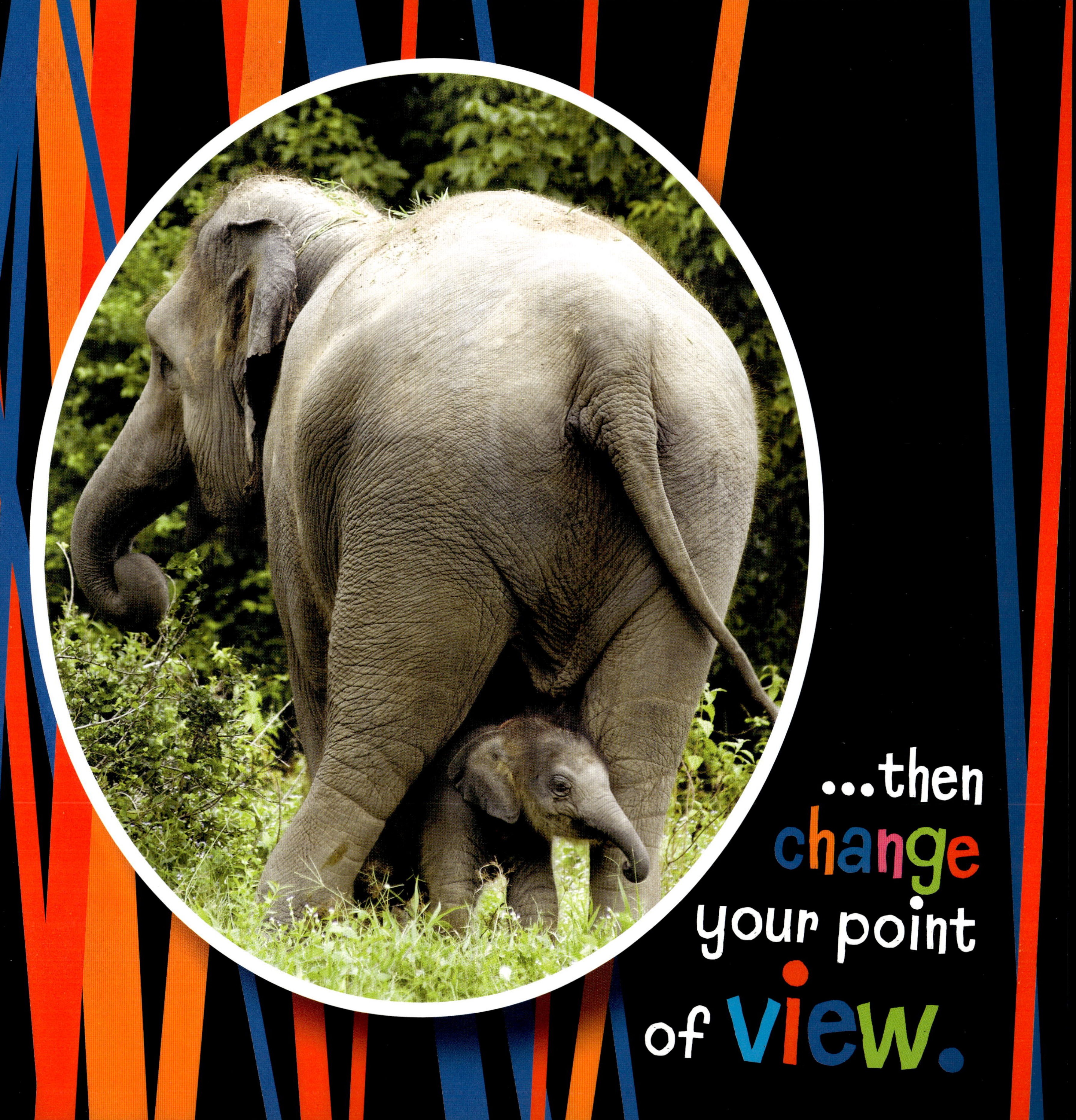

...then change your point of view.

Try not to think of just yourself.

Invent new ways to share.

Stay close to friends whom you can trust.

But
always
be
aware.

Avoid the tattle in the tale.

Insist that **truth** is **best.**

Embrace with pride
the strengths you have.

Demand to be impressed.

Enjoy the peace that nature brings.

Ignore what's just for show.

Join forces when the road gets rough.

Admit when you don't know.

Remember family is the best.

Despite the ups and downs.

Don't hide from things that you must face.

Make joyful laughing sounds.

Eat healthy food to grow up strong.

Be patient with your friends.

Try not to take a stubborn stand.

Be
quick
to make
amends.

Excuse yourself when manners slip.

Be helpful every day.

Keep trying
even when it's hard.

But
don't
forget to
play!

And sing

... and dance each day!

Written by Kate B. Jerome
Design and Production: Lumina Datamatics, Inc.
Coloring Illustrations: Tom Pounders
Research: Eric Nyquist

Cover Images: See back cover

Interior Images: 002 Anetapics/Shutterstock.com; 003 George Green/Shutterstock.com; 004 Sergey Uryadnikov/Shutterstock.com; 005 Gnomeandi/Shutterstock.com; 006 Bruce MacQueen/Shutterstock.com; 007 Henk Bentlage/Shutterstock.com; 008 M.M./Shutterstock.com; 009 Mikael Damkier/Shutterstock.com; 010 Brendan van Son/Shutterstock.com; 011 Michael Pettigrew/Shutterstock.com; 012 StevenRussellSmithPhotos/Shutterstock.com; 013 Pakhnyushchy/Shutterstock.com; 014 Patjo/Shutterstock.com; 015 Quinn Martin/Shutterstock.com; 016 Lincoln Rogers/Shutterstock.com; 017 Dirk Ercken/Shutterstock.com; 018 Karel Gallas/Shutterstock.com; 019 Orangecrush/Shutterstock.com; 020 Guenter-foto/Shutterstock.com; 021 Janecat/Shutterstock.com; 022 Shironina/Shutterstock.com; 023 Annette Shaff/Shutterstock.com; 024 Vitaly Titov/Shutterstock.com; 025 Rohappy/Shutterstock.com; 026 MattiaATH/Shutterstock.com; 027 Otsphoto/Shutterstock.com; 028 FikMik/Shutterstock.com; 029 Four Oaks/Shutterstock.com; 030 Ekaterina Kolomeets/Shutterstock.com; 031 Hugh Lansdown/Shutterstock.com.

Published by Arcadia Kids, a division of Arcadia Publishing and The History Press, Charleston, SC

For all general information contact Arcadia Publishing at:
Telephone: 843-853-2070
Email: sales@arcadiapublishing.com

For Customer Service and Orders:
Toll Free: 1-888-313-2665
Visit us on the Internet at www.arcadiapublishing.com

Library of Congress Cataloging-in-Publication data is on file with the publisher.

Printed in China

Nevada State Bird

Mountain Bluebird

Read Together

Citizens and schoolchildren across the state voted for the mountain bluebird to be the state bird in 1931, but it wasn't signed into law until 1967!

Nevada State Reptile

Desert Tortoise

Read Together

The desert tortoise was named the state reptile in 1989. They live in the southern desert area of Nevada where they spend most of their time in underground burrows to escape the heat.

Nevada State Insect

Vivid Dancer Damselfly

Read Together

The vivid dancer damselfly was named the state insect in 2009. Fourth grade students from across the state entered a contest to describe their pick for state insect. The winning essay came from John R. Beatty Elementary School in Las Vegas.

Nevada State Animal

Desert Bighorn Sheep

Read Together

The desert bighorn sheep was named the state animal in 1973. The sheep can be found in Nevada's rocky desert.